Memodoo

Memorable
CONCERTS

This Memodoo is an easy and fun
way to enjoy and relive
your memories of concerts
you have gone to

CONFETTI PUBLISHING

Memodoo Memorable Concerts

www.confettipublishing.com

For translations, licensing of the Memodoo brand, co-branded Memodoo editions, and
bulk purchase, please contact publisher@confettipublishing.com

Series editor: Henrik Vejlgaard

ISBN 978-1-939235-07-7

This Memodoo belongs to

_____

CONTENT

Foreword

How to Memodoo

Memodoo Titles

30 Entries with Cues

About Memodoo

FOREWORD

Welcome to a whole new way of systematizing the memorable moments of your life. We call it Memodooing!

Memories are an important part of a rich and fulfilling life. We all have them. Often a keepsake or photograph can bring back memories. But neither a keepsake nor photographs can give the full story of a particular memory because in spite of our best intentions, we forget our feelings and thoughts—and quite a few details. That is why it is important to Memodoo—to systematically keep track of the memorable moments of your life by writing them down in your Memodoo.

Nowadays a lot of people use social media to write about many aspects of their life. Even though we document our life in social media it is not very systematic and it is not the easiest way to get an overview of the memorable moments of your life. With one or more Memodoos you will always have a systematic and easy overview of all your memorable experiences.

A Memodoo consists of pages with pre-printed, easy-to-use cues that you fill out in order to keep track of your memories. Memodooing is about writing down the key words that will trigger your memory of special experiences. But Memodoos are not only about writing down facts, they are also about rating, reviewing, and reflecting on experiences—in other words, expressing how you felt.

We have different Memodoos for all the situations when you will be happy that personal experiences are not just stored casually in your memory but also systematically in your Memodoo.

With Memodoo we also introduce a new way of talking about our memories. Memodoo (pronounced memo<u>DOOOO</u>) is an innovative addition to our language because it makes it easier to talk about what our memories mean to us. This is because Memodoo is a triple-duty word. It can be a noun: a Memodoo means "a personal book to systematically record, rate, and review one's experiences." It can also be a verb: to Memodoo (or Memodooing) means "systemizing one's memories of different experiences in a Memodoo." Or as an adjective, for instance: a Memodoo experience, which means "an experience that is worth writing down in a Memodoo."

You have more than 30 different Memodoos from which you can choose. In other words, you can create a collection of Memodoos that precisely matches your life and your experiences. Then you are a Memodoo'er!

As a Memodoo'er you are bound to find much more pleasure in your experiences because you will enjoy them when you experience them, and also when you write them down and then again when you go back to read and relive them in your Memodoo.

HOW TO MEMODOO

Memodoos keep track of all the memorable experiences of your life in a clear and systematic way. With your Memodoo you always have a systematic overview of your memorable experiences.

In a Memodoo you will never be intimidated by a blank page–because there are no blank pages in a Memodoo. Each page is filled with printed cues that will guide you in your writing and get around the experience.

Keep It Brief

Keep your writing brief. Just write enough to trigger your memory when you want to relive an experience by reading about it in your Memodoo. Also, you do not have to fill out the entire entry–just what you find relevant. Sometimes you can just put + for something positive and - for something negative.

Recording Facts

You can record the facts of your experience in a Memodoo. If you and your family, friends, and colleagues have lapses of memory you can always consult your Memodoo, and if you remember things differently from someone else you can always consult your Memodoo to get the facts right.

Remembering Thoughts and Feelings

Many of the cues give you the opportunity to write down feelings and thoughts. Writing your thoughts and feelings down it often ground for reflections that can give an extra dimension to your experience.

Reviewing

You can use a Memodoo to express your opinions–and be as creative as you feel like. You can be a reviewer and write down your opinion–just like a reviewer at a newspaper or magazine. When you want to share your opinion on a subject written down in a Memodoo you can always consult your Memodoo reviews.

Rating

Newspapers, magazines, restaurant guides etc. use points or scales to rate everything from books to restaurants. You, too, can do that in the Memodoos. This kind of rating not only makes it easy to summarize your opinion but also makes it easy to find the very best experiences, when you browse through your Memodoo. A star rating is one of the popular ways of rating. You can for instance use this five star rating scale:

*	Disappointing experience
**	OK experience
***	Nice experience
****	Great experience
*****	Exceptional and unique experience

You can also give points from 1-10. You can, of course, also create your own way of rating.

MEMORABLE QUOTES

"My diaries were written not to preserve the experience, but to savour it, to make it even more real, more visible and palpable, than in actual life. For in our family an experience was not finished, unless written down."

—*Anne Morrow Lindbergh* (American author and aviator)

"A diary need not be a dreary chronicle of one's movements; it should aim rather at giving a salient account of some particular episode, a walk, a book, a conversation."

–*A.C. Benson* (English poet)

Memodoo TITLES

- Memorable Art Shows
- Memorable Birthdays
- Memorable Books
- Memorable Concerts
- Memorable Conversations
- Memorable Cooking
- Memorable Dating
- Memorable Dinner Parties
- Memorable Dreams
- Memorable Family Gatherings
- Memorable Holidays
- Memorable Love Affairs
- Memorable Matches in Sport
- Memorable Moments as a Parent
- Memorable Moments of Happiness
- Memorable Moments with Pets
- Memorable Movies
- Memorable Museum Visits
- Memorable Nature Sights
- Memorable Parties
- Memorable Religious Ceremonies
- Memorable Restaurants
- Memorable Sex
- Memorable Shopping
- Memorable Spiritual Moments
- Memorable Television
- Memorable Theatre
- Memorable Tourist Attractions
- Memorable Wine
- Memorable Years

30 Entries with Cues

Date: _____

Title of concert/tour: _____

Artist(s) performing: _____

_____

_____

Venue: _____

City: _____

Companion(s): _____

_____

_____

Seating: _____

Music performed: _____

_____

_____

What I liked: _____

_____

_____

What I did not like: _____

_____

_____

Highlight: _____

_____

_____

My opinion of the concert: _____

_____

_____

Other people's opinion of the concert: _____

_____

_____

_____

Overall rating: _____

Social activities before/after concert: _____

_____

_____

Date: _____

Title of concert/tour: _____

Artist(s) performing: _____

_____

_____

Venue: _____

City: _____

Companion(s): _____

_____

_____

Seating: _____

Music performed: _____

_____

_____

What I liked: _____

_____

_____

What I did not like: _____

_____

_____

Highlight: _____

_____

_____

My opinion of the concert: _____

_____

_____

Other people's opinion of the concert: _____

_____

_____

_____

Overall rating: _____

Social activities before/after concert: _____

_____

_____

Date: _____

Title of concert/tour: _____

Artist(s) performing: _____

_____

_____

Venue: _____

City: _____

Companion(s): _____

_____

_____

Seating: _____

Music performed: _____

_____

_____

What I liked: _____

_____

_____

What I did not like: _____

_____

_____

Highlight: _____

_____

_____

My opinion of the concert: _____

_____

_____

Other people's opinion of the concert: _____

_____

_____

_____

Overall rating: _____

Social activities before/after concert: _____

_____

_____

Date: _____

Title of concert/tour: _____

Artist(s) performing: _____

_____

_____

Venue: _____

City: _____

Companion(s): _____

_____

_____

Seating: _____

Music performed: _____

_____

_____

What I liked: _____

_____

_____

What I did not like: _____

_____

_____

Highlight: _____

_____

_____

My opinion of the concert: _____

_____

_____

Other people's opinion of the concert: _____

_____

_____

_____

Overall rating: _____

Social activities before/after concert: _____

_____

_____

Date: _____

Title of concert/tour: _____

Artist(s) performing: _____

_____

_____

Venue: _____

City: _____

Companion(s): _____

_____

_____

Seating: _____

Music performed: _____

_____

_____

What I liked: _____

_____

_____

What I did not like: _____

_____

_____

Highlight: _____

_____

_____

My opinion of the concert: _____

_____

_____

Other people's opinion of the concert: _____

_____

_____

_____

Overall rating: _____

Social activities before/after concert: _____

_____

_____

Date: _____

Title of concert/tour: _____

Artist(s) performing: _____

_____

_____

Venue: _____

City: _____

Companion(s): _____

_____

_____

Seating: _____

Music performed: _____

_____

_____

What I liked: _____

_____

_____

What I did not like: _____

_____

_____

Highlight: _____

_____

_____

My opinion of the concert: _____

_____

_____

Other people's opinion of the concert: _____

_____

_____

_____

Overall rating: _____

Social activities before/after concert: _____

_____

_____

Date: _____

Title of concert/tour: _____

Artist(s) performing: _____

_____

_____

Venue: _____

City: _____

Companion(s): _____

_____

_____

Seating: _____

Music performed: _____

_____

_____

What I liked: _____

_____

_____

What I did not like: _____

_____

_____

Highlight: _____

_____

_____

My opinion of the concert: _____

_____

_____

Other people's opinion of the concert: _____

_____

_____

_____

Overall rating: _____

Social activities before/after concert: _____

_____

_____

Date: _____

Title of concert/tour: _____

Artist(s) performing: _____

_____

_____

Venue: _____

City: _____

Companion(s): _____

_____

_____

Seating: _____

Music performed: _____

_____

_____

What I liked: _____

_____

_____

What I did not like: _____

_____

_____

Highlight: _____

_____

_____

My opinion of the concert: _____

_____

_____

Other people's opinion of the concert: _____

_____

_____

_____

Overall rating: _____

Social activities before/after concert: _____

_____

_____

Date: _____

Title of concert/tour: _____

Artist(s) performing: _____

_____

_____

Venue: _____

City: _____

Companion(s): _____

_____

_____

Seating: _____

Music performed: _____

_____

_____

What I liked: _____

_____

_____

What I did not like: _____

_____

_____

Highlight: _____

_____

_____

My opinion of the concert: _____

_____

_____

Other people's opinion of the concert: _____

_____

_____

_____

Overall rating: _____

Social activities before/after concert: _____

_____

_____

Date: _____

Title of concert/tour: _____

Artist(s) performing: _____

_____

_____

Venue: _____

City: _____

Companion(s): _____

_____

_____

Seating: _____

Music performed: _____

_____

_____

What I liked: _____

_____

_____

What I did not like: _____

_____

_____

Highlight: _____

_____

_____

My opinion of the concert: _____

_____

_____

Other people's opinion of the concert: _____

_____

_____

_____

Overall rating: _____

Social activities before/after concert: _____

_____

_____

Date: _____

Title of concert/tour: _____

Artist(s) performing: _____

_____

_____

Venue: _____

City: _____

Companion(s): _____

_____

_____

Seating: _____

Music performed: _____

_____

_____

What I liked: _____

_____

_____

What I did not like: _____

_____

_____

Highlight: _____

_____

_____

My opinion of the concert: _____

_____

_____

Other people's opinion of the concert: _____

_____

_____

_____

Overall rating: _____

Social activities before/after concert: _____

_____

_____

Date: _____

Title of concert/tour: _____

Artist(s) performing: _____

_____

_____

Venue: _____

City: _____

Companion(s): _____

_____

_____

Seating: _____

Music performed: _____

_____

_____

What I liked: _____

_____

_____

What I did not like: _____

_____

_____

Highlight: _____

_____

_____

My opinion of the concert: _____

_____

_____

Other people's opinion of the concert: _____

_____

_____

_____

Overall rating: _____

Social activities before/after concert: _____

_____

_____

Date: _____

Title of concert/tour: _____

Artist(s) performing: _____

_____

_____

Venue: _____

City: _____

Companion(s): _____

_____

_____

Seating: _____

Music performed: _____

_____

_____

What I liked: _____

_____

_____

What I did not like: _____

_____

_____

Highlight: _____

_____

_____

My opinion of the concert: _____

_____

_____

Other people's opinion of the concert: _____

_____

_____

_____

Overall rating: _____

Social activities before/after concert: _____

_____

_____

Date: _____

Title of concert/tour: _____

Artist(s) performing: _____

_____

_____

Venue: _____

City: _____

Companion(s): _____

_____

_____

Seating: _____

Music performed: _____

_____

_____

What I liked: _____

_____

_____

What I did not like: _____

_____

_____

Highlight: _____

_____

_____

My opinion of the concert: _____

_____

_____

Other people's opinion of the concert: _____

_____

_____

_____

Overall rating: _____

Social activities before/after concert: _____

_____

_____

Date: _____

Title of concert/tour: _____

Artist(s) performing: _____

_____

_____

Venue: _____

City: _____

Companion(s): _____

_____

_____

Seating: _____

Music performed: _____

_____

_____

What I liked: _____

_____

_____

What I did not like: _____

_____

_____

Highlight: _____

_____

_____

My opinion of the concert: _____

_____

_____

Other people's opinion of the concert: _____

_____

_____

_____

Overall rating: _____

Social activities before/after concert: _____

_____

_____

Date: _____

Title of concert/tour: _____

Artist(s) performing: _____

_____

_____

Venue: _____

City: _____

Companion(s): _____

_____

_____

Seating: _____

Music performed: _____

_____

_____

What I liked: _____

_____

_____

What I did not like: _____

_____

_____

Highlight: _____

_____

_____

My opinion of the concert: _____

_____

_____

Other people's opinion of the concert: _____

_____

_____

_____

Overall rating: _____

Social activities before/after concert: _____

_____

_____

Date: _____

Title of concert/tour: _____

Artist(s) performing: _____

_____

_____

Venue: _____

City: _____

Companion(s): _____

_____

_____

Seating: _____

Music performed: _____

_____

_____

What I liked: _____

_____

_____

What I did not like: _____

_____

_____

Highlight: _____

_____

_____

My opinion of the concert: _____

_____

_____

Other people's opinion of the concert: _____

_____

_____

_____

Overall rating: _____

Social activities before/after concert: _____

_____

_____

Date: _____

Title of concert/tour: _____

Artist(s) performing: _____

_____

_____

Venue: _____

City: _____

Companion(s): _____

_____

_____

Seating: _____

Music performed: _____

_____

_____

What I liked: _____

_____

_____

What I did not like: _____

_____

_____

Highlight: _____

_____

_____

My opinion of the concert: _____

_____

_____

Other people's opinion of the concert: _____

_____

_____

_____

Overall rating: _____

Social activities before/after concert: _____

_____

_____

Date: _____

Title of concert/tour: _____

Artist(s) performing: _____

_____

_____

Venue: _____

City: _____

Companion(s): _____

_____

_____

Seating: _____

Music performed: _____

_____

_____

What I liked: _____

_____

_____

What I did not like: _____

_____

_____

Highlight: _____

_____

_____

My opinion of the concert: _____

_____

_____

Other people's opinion of the concert: _____

_____

_____

_____

Overall rating: _____

Social activities before/after concert: _____

_____

_____

Date: _____

Title of concert/tour: _____

Artist(s) performing: _____

_____

_____

Venue: _____

City: _____

Companion(s): _____

_____

_____

Seating: _____

Music performed: _____

_____

_____

What I liked: _____

_____

_____

What I did not like: _____

_____

_____

Highlight: _____

_____

_____

My opinion of the concert: _____

_____

_____

Other people's opinion of the concert: _____

_____

_____

_____

Overall rating: _____

Social activities before/after concert: _____

_____

_____

Date: _____

Title of concert/tour: _____

Artist(s) performing: _____

_____

_____

Venue: _____

City: _____

Companion(s): _____

_____

_____

Seating: _____

Music performed: _____

_____

_____

What I liked: _____

_____

_____

What I did not like: _____

_____

_____

Highlight: _____

_____

_____

My opinion of the concert: _____

_____

_____

Other people's opinion of the concert: _____

_____

_____

_____

Overall rating: _____

Social activities before/after concert: _____

_____

_____

Date: _____

Title of concert/tour: _____

Artist(s) performing: _____

_____

_____

Venue: _____

City: _____

Companion(s): _____

_____

_____

Seating: _____

Music performed: _____

_____

_____

What I liked: _____

_____

_____

What I did not like: _____

_____

_____

Highlight: _____

_____

_____

My opinion of the concert: _____

_____

_____

Other people's opinion of the concert: _____

_____

_____

_____

Overall rating: _____

Social activities before/after concert: _____

_____

_____

Date: _____

Title of concert/tour: _____

Artist(s) performing: _____

_____

_____

Venue: _____

City: _____

Companion(s): _____

_____

_____

Seating: _____

Music performed: _____

_____

_____

What I liked: _____

_____

_____

What I did not like: _____

_____

_____

Highlight: _____

_____

_____

My opinion of the concert: _____

_____

_____

Other people's opinion of the concert: _____

_____

_____

_____

Overall rating: _____

Social activities before/after concert: _____

_____

_____

Date: _____

Title of concert/tour: _____

Artist(s) performing: _____

_____

_____

Venue: _____

City: _____

Companion(s): _____

_____

_____

Seating: _____

Music performed: _____

_____

_____

What I liked: _____

_____

_____

What I did not like: _____

_____

_____

Highlight: _____

_____

_____

My opinion of the concert: _____

_____

_____

Other people's opinion of the concert: _____

_____

_____

_____

Overall rating: _____

Social activities before/after concert: _____

_____

_____

Date: _____

Title of concert/tour: _____

Artist(s) performing: _____

_____

_____

Venue: _____

City: _____

Companion(s): _____

_____

_____

Seating: _____

Music performed: _____

_____

_____

What I liked: _____

_____

_____

What I did not like: _____

_____

_____

Highlight: _____

_____

_____

My opinion of the concert: _____

_____

_____

Other people's opinion of the concert: _____

_____

_____

_____

Overall rating: _____

Social activities before/after concert: _____

_____

_____

Date: _____

Title of concert/tour: _____

Artist(s) performing: _____

_____

_____

Venue: _____

City: _____

Companion(s): _____

_____

_____

Seating: _____

Music performed: _____

_____

_____

What I liked: _____

_____

_____

What I did not like: _____

_____

_____

Highlight: _____

_____

_____

My opinion of the concert: _____

_____

_____

Other people's opinion of the concert: _____

_____

_____

_____

Overall rating: _____

Social activities before/after concert: _____

_____

_____

Date: _____

Title of concert/tour: _____

Artist(s) performing: _____

_____

_____

Venue: _____

City: _____

Companion(s): _____

_____

_____

Seating: _____

Music performed: _____

_____

_____

What I liked: _____

_____

_____

What I did not like: _____

_____

_____

Highlight: _____

_____

_____

My opinion of the concert: _____

_____

_____

Other people's opinion of the concert: _____

_____

_____

_____

Overall rating: _____

Social activities before/after concert: _____

_____

_____

Date: _____

Title of concert/tour: _____

Artist(s) performing: _____

_____

_____

Venue: _____

City: _____

Companion(s): _____

_____

_____

Seating: _____

Music performed: _____

_____

_____

What I liked: _____

_____

_____

What I did not like: _____

_____

_____

Highlight: _____

_____

_____

My opinion of the concert: _____

_____

_____

Other people's opinion of the concert: _____

_____

_____

_____

Overall rating: _____

Social activities before/after concert: _____

_____

_____

Date: _____

Title of concert/tour: _____

Artist(s) performing: _____

_____

_____

Venue: _____

City: _____

Companion(s): _____

_____

_____

Seating: _____

Music performed: _____

_____

_____

What I liked: _____

_____

_____

What I did not like: _____

_____

_____

Highlight: _____

_____

_____

My opinion of the concert: _____

_____

_____

Other people's opinion of the concert: _____

_____

_____

_____

Overall rating: _____

Social activities before/after concert: _____

_____

_____

Date: _____

Title of concert/tour: _____

Artist(s) performing: _____

_____

_____

Venue: _____

City: _____

Companion(s): _____

_____

_____

Seating: _____

Music performed: _____

_____

_____

What I liked: _____

_____

_____

What I did not like: _____

_____

_____

Highlight: _____

_____

_____

My opinion of the concert: _____

_____

_____

Other people's opinion of the concert: _____

_____

_____

_____

Overall rating: _____

Social activities before/after concert: _____

_____

_____

Date: _____

Title of concert/tour: _____

Artist(s) performing: _____

_____

_____

Venue: _____

City: _____

Companion(s): _____

_____

_____

Seating: _____

Music performed: _____

_____

_____

What I liked: _____

_____

_____

What I did not like: _____

_____

_____

Highlight: _____

_____

_____

My opinion of the concert: _____

_____

_____

Other people's opinion of the concert: _____

_____

_____

_____

Overall rating: _____

Social activities before/after concert: _____

_____

_____

It is time to buy a new Memodoo to remember, rate, and review more experiences. You can get these Memodoos:

- Memorable Art Shows
- Memorable Birthdays
- Memorable Books
- Memorable Concerts
- Memorable Conversations
- Memorable Cooking
- Memorable Dating
- Memorable Dinner Parties
- Memorable Dreams
- Memorable Family Gatherings
- Memorable Holidays
- Memorable Love Affairs
- Memorable Matches in Sport
- Memorable Moments as a Parent
- Memorable Moments of Happiness
- Memorable Moments with Pets
- Memorable Movies
- Memorable Museum Visits
- Memorable Nature Sights
- Memorable Parties
- Memorable Religious Ceremonies
- Memorable Restaurants
- Memorable Sex
- Memorable Shopping
- Memorable Spiritual Moments
- Memorable Television
- Memorable Theatre
- Memorable Tourist Attractions
- Memorable Wine
- Memorable Years

ABOUT Memodoo

Memodoo is the brainchild of Henrik Vejlgaard, M.A., M.Sc., who has written *Anatomy of a Trend* and several other books about trends, identity and lifestyles. Writing about these subjects certainly makes you aware of all the changes that take place in today's world, and also the importance of our identity.

In many ways our identity is defined by past experiences, but as we unfortunately also tend to forget the details of these experiences, Henrik realized that we need a tool to systematically keep track of our past experiences. With this back story he created the Memodoos that can help not only to systemize our memories but also to strengthen our identity.

There are more than 30 different Memodoos that Henrik has created by carefully studying all aspects of present-day identity in his book *The Lifestyle Puzzle*. Depending upon the life you lead you can pick and mix the Memodoos that match your experiences.

www.memodoo.com

Join us on

Facebook.com/Memodoo